THE BOOK OF FANTASTIC BOATS

Illustrated by
ROY COOMBS

Written by
CHRISTINE BERNARD

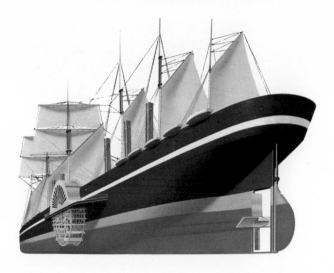

Copyright © 1974 The Archon Press Limited, London
U.S. edition published 1974 by Golden Press, New York. Western Publishing Company, Inc. Printed in U.S.A.
All rights reserved. Golden, A Golden Book ®, and Golden Press ® are trademarks of Western Publishing Company, Inc.
Library of Congress Catalog Card Number: 73-92284
ISBN: 0 307 12677 3

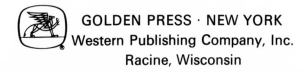

GOLDEN PRESS · NEW YORK
Western Publishing Company, Inc.
Racine, Wisconsin

INTRODUCTION

From earliest times, man has found ways of crossing water by means of floating logs and simple craft. As soon as he learned to use tools, he was able to hollow out tree trunks and shape them into canoes. Other kinds of boats were made of animal skins, reeds, and bark.

At first, these boats were propelled by paddles and oars. Then man learned to take advantage of the wind and used primitive sails. These first small boats were used on hunting expeditions and fishing trips. But, as time went on, man grew more adventurous and embarked on longer and longer sailing journeys across the seas.

Sometimes men were driven to take to the sea in search of new lands on which to settle. Such was the plight of the ancient Polynesians who left their islands in the South Pacific. They built the strongest boats they knew how to and set sail with their destination unknown. New Zealand was among the many islands eventually peopled by these brave sailors and their families over three thousand years ago.

The ancient Egyptians were also skilled boat builders. Their small river boats were made of papyrus reeds bound together and made watertight with pitch. They were river people who worshipped the mighty Nile River as a great god because it flooded their lands and fertilized their fields. In such a geographical area, their sailing boats proved to be invaluable.

Of all the ancient seafaring peoples, the ones most often remembered are the Vikings. In their longboats, these daring men from Scandinavia were the fiercest pirates of the high seas. They were fearless fighters and superb seamen who made tremendous voyages in their remarkable boats. Some Vikings even crossed the entire Atlantic Ocean and landed in Canada and America.

There was a very long gap in time before mankind found other means than the oar and sail to propel himself over water. Not until 1787 did an American engineer invent another method: he designed a boat that was driven by ejecting water from the stern of the boat. Steam and motor powered boats followed soon after, although many such boats were also equipped with sails. The Great Eastern, for instance, still carried large sails even though it was powered by steam engines and huge paddle wheels. However, steam slowly took over completely and the unusual Cigar Ship and astonishing Popoffkas appeared.

By the turn of the twentieth century, masts disappeared and even steam engines were vanishing because of the great diesel engines that powered many great giants of the sea like the Globtik Tokyo. Nevertheless, steam is still used very much today as evidenced by the USS Enterprise, which relies on steam turbines driven by steam created by nuclear power.

Today's most modern Crossbow, Hydrofoil and Hovercraft are boats of intriguing style that exemplify man's desire to travel faster and with less effort over the water, and this book shows them all.

Some words that may be unfamiliar are explained in the glossary at the back of this book.

MAORI TAINUI about A.D. 1300

Country: South Pacific Islands. **Size:** over 70 ft. long.
It was one of the first outrigger canoes.

In ships like these, some of the people of the Pacific islands made their voyages across the South Pacific. Known today as Maoris, these people settled on the islands they discovered, among them the islands known as New Zealand. Even when at sea, their tribal customs were maintained. The chief and his men slept in the wooden cabin, which was supported by crossbeams between the two canoes, where the women and children slept. The extraordinary sails were shaped to catch the wind and for many centuries this craft provided sea transport for the Maoris. As recently as 1770, Captain Cook on one of his voyages noted that a Tainui had 'great elegance'.

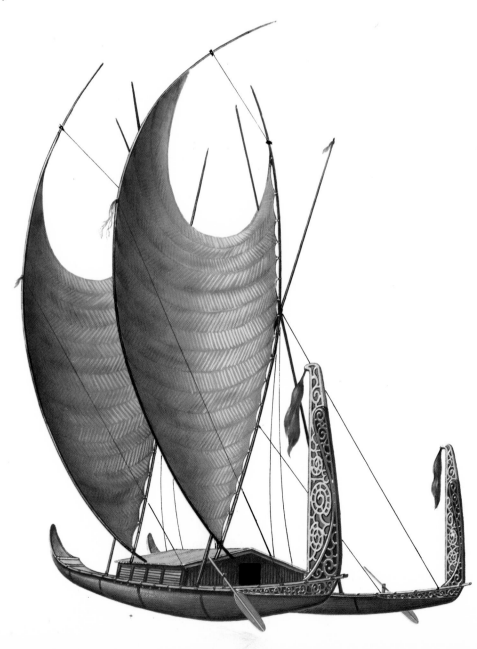

RA 2000 B.C.

Country: Egypt.
Size: 40 ft. long,
16 ft. wide, 6 ft. deep,
cabin 12 ft. × 9 ft.
**It was one of the
earliest ocean-
going boats.**

The Egyptians are known to have been great naval architects and they travelled great distances in their vessels, perhaps as far as South America. Ra himself was the Egyptian god of the sun. By day, according to the legend, he travelled across the sky in his boat, and at night he boarded another boat to make his dangerous journey through the underworld. There he had frequent battles with Apep, the serpent of darkness. Needless to say, Ra was always the victor and rose to continue his journey the next day. Thor Heyerdahl, a Norwegian writer and explorer, reconstructed one of these beautiful Egyptian ships calling it Ra, after the great sun god of the Egyptians. From ancient writings it has been learned that these ships had no keel, no post at each end and no frame at all. Papyrus stalks were plaited together and bound over a wooden dugout, to give protection against the ocean seas.

ROMAN BIREME 30 B.C.

Country: Rome. **Size:** about 65 ft. long.
It was the warship the Romans used on their conquests.

No remains of this boat have ever been found, but scholars have managed to piece together some facts from ancient mosaics and carvings. It is known, for instance, that the Romans followed Greek designs, and that the first 'bireme'—called this because of its two banks of oars—was built during the 7th century B.C. in Greece. Although the Roman one in this picture is of a later date, it was similar in size and appearance, and highly decorated with beautiful wood carvings.

The bireme was propelled by rows of oarsmen, usually slaves or criminals chained to their benches, and part of the wooden deck was left open to allow them air. The tower, which looks more suitable for land than sea, was used only during combat—perhaps as a protection against flying spears—and was probably of wood painted to look like stone. The ship's chief weapon of war, the horrific three-pronged spear positioned below the prow, presented a fearsome sight and was used to ram and sink the enemy.

VIKING LONGBOAT about A.D. 1000

Country: Scandinavia.
Size: up to 150 ft. long.
It was the fighting ship of the Viking conquerors.

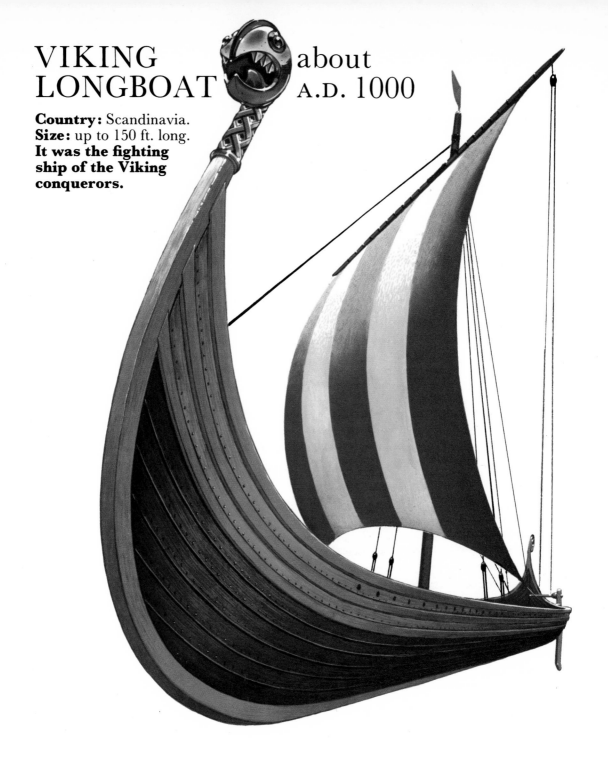

Legends tell how these beautiful boats carried Nordic kings, in particular Eric the Red and his son Leif, on their voyages of exploration. It is from these sources and the Bayeux Tapestries in France that accurate descriptions of these longboats have been put together. Powered by up to 60 oarsmen, they were strong enough to brave the dangerous seas of the North Atlantic where storms and ice floes continually threatened. The carved dragon's head on the prow was only carried on voyages of war and raiding expeditions. Royal ships with their multicolored linen sails, many of which were embroidered in silk, must have been a magnificent sight.

PORTUGUESE MULETA
from A.D. 1000 to A.D. 1900

Country: Portugal. **Size:** 50 ft. long, 12 ft. wide.
It could set its sails to drift sideways when trawling.

The Phoenicians were among the earliest people to build and navigate sea-going vessels, and it is from these people that the Portuguese fisherfolk claim descent. The Muleta, with its curved stem, painted eyes and shaped bows, was just like an ancient Phoenician boat, while the ornamental strips round the hull were similar to those on early Greek ships.
Just as the appearance was unusual so was the Muleta's method of trawling. Sailing with the tide down to the river mouth, the fishermen would lay the trawls and then drift back upstream with the wind and returning tide. With all its heavy sails set, the boat returned sideways.
The Portuguese used the Muleta for some nine centuries. With the increasing river traffic and the arrival of steam boats, however, they became a danger to other craft and, by the end of the 19th century, they were no longer used.

IRAWADI RICE BOAT
A.D. 1000 to present

Country: Burma. **Size:** approx. 80–100 ft. long.
It has been used for transport for nearly 1,000 years.

This boat was built to carry passengers and merchandise in Burma. From the first ancient crude dug-out canoe, it has developed into a large picturesque sailing boat. Its fairy-tale beauty gives it a fragile appearance, but over the centuries it has proved to be a very useful and reliable craft. The hull is still basically a dug-out canoe, which is first soaked to make it flexible and then stretched to its final shape. The strange, looped sails are delicately balanced to catch the breezes of the Irawadi, the huge river that runs through Burma, and the boat is steered by a side rudder. The long deckhouse (not unlike the dry land homes of the Burmese people) is thatched with palm, and the stern of the boat is decorated with intricate carvings and paintings.

TURTLE 1776

Country: U.S.A. **Size:** approx. 7 ft. high, 4 ft. wide, keel to conning tower 8 ft.
It was the earliest submarine.

This earliest recorded submarine was built by Captain David Bushnell of Connecticut. It was made of oak and constructed in two halves joined together, with a brass 'conning tower' at the top. To allow the submarine to submerge, water was let into ballast tanks through valves and for re-surfacing a hand-operated mechanism pumped out the water. The two large propellers set at different angles were turned by hand and controlled the craft under water. The purpose of the Turtle was to blow up enemy ships, and the special screw attached to the explosive charge carried in the red box was designed to bore into the bottom of the enemy boat, leaving behind the explosive. Captain Bushnell's invention failed because the screw was useless against the copper-covered keels of the boats of the time.

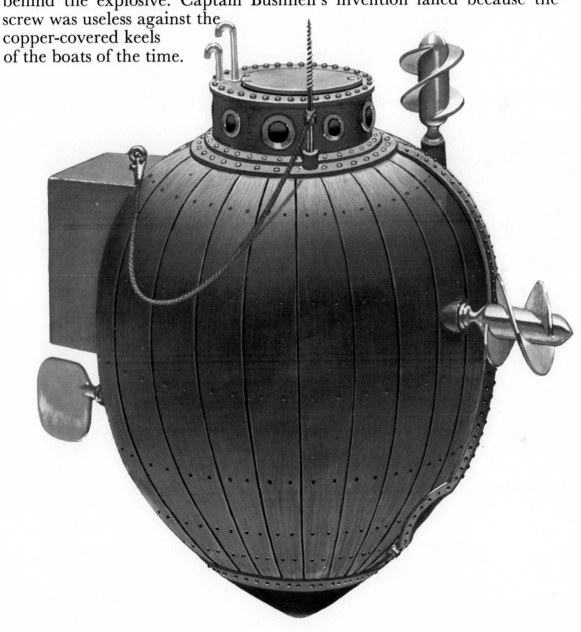

CIGAR SHIP 1858

Country: U.S.A. **Size:** 180 ft. long, 16 ft. in diameter.
It looked like a cigar.

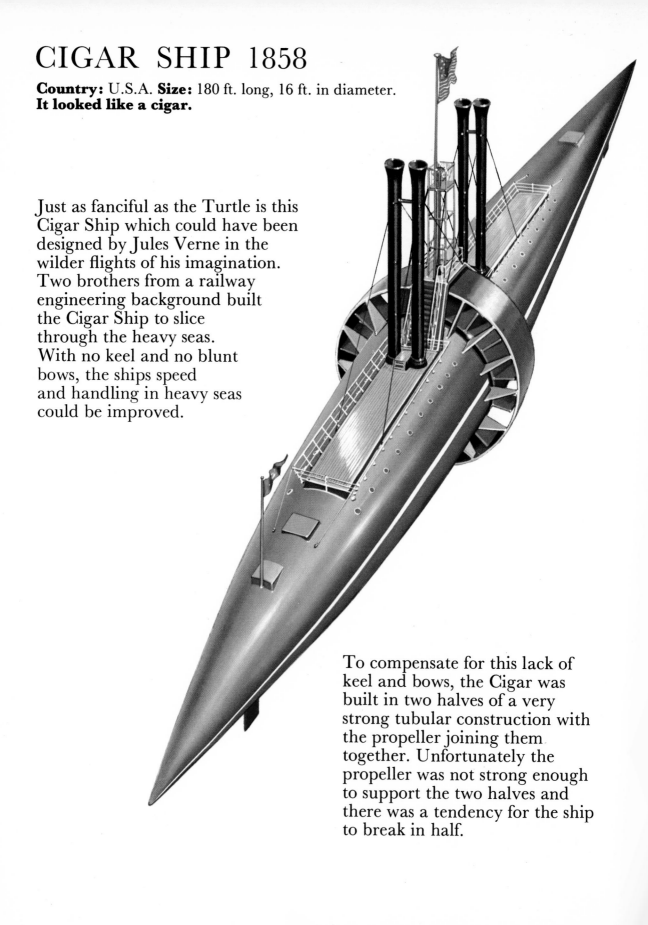

Just as fanciful as the Turtle is this Cigar Ship which could have been designed by Jules Verne in the wilder flights of his imagination. Two brothers from a railway engineering background built the Cigar Ship to slice through the heavy seas. With no keel and no blunt bows, the ships speed and handling in heavy seas could be improved.

To compensate for this lack of keel and bows, the Cigar was built in two halves of a very strong tubular construction with the propeller joining them together. Unfortunately the propeller was not strong enough to support the two halves and there was a tendency for the ship to break in half.

CONNECTOR or
JOINTED SHIP 1858

Country: Great Britain. **Size:** approx. 150 ft. long.
It was built as three or four separate ships.

There is no official detailed account to be found of this Jointed Ship, so only eyewitness descriptions tell of this fascinating invention. Built in three or four sections, the object of the Connector's hinges was two-fold: to enable the ship to ride rough seas more easily with no risk of breaking her back, and to enable each of the sections to separate from the others, the fore and aft sections providing the power as well as the protection. Once separated, each of the middle sections could make its own way inshore. An observer at the time commented, 'Each section is a perfect portion of the hull, capable of being disconnected with perfect ease, almost in a few seconds . . .'

Designed to carry coal from the north of England to London, the fate of the Connector is not known.

GREAT EASTERN 1858

Country: Great Britain. **Size:** 692 ft. long, 120 ft. wide.
For fifty years this was the largest ship in the world.

This great iron ship was planned by the famous British engineer,
Isambard Kingdom Brunel. His earlier ship, the Great Western, had
missed, by only a few hours, being the first steamer to cross
the Atlantic. The Great Eastern broke many records: she was
twice as big as her nearest rival, the largest ship in the
world for 50 years, and the only one to have both
paddlewheels and propellers. Carrying 12,000 tons
of coal, apart from her huge cargo and 4,000
passengers, she could travel as far as
Australia without refuelling.
Sadly, this ship must have been
launched under an unlucky star.
Deaths, accidents and
disasters haunted her career.
The ship was expensive to
run, and the design so
complex that there was
always a shortage of crew
skilled enough to operate
her. After 11 years of
near inactivity she
suffered the indignity
of becoming a floating
amusement park. Finally,
in 1888, she was towed
off to the scrap heap
but her hull was so
strong that it took three
years to demolish!

POPOFFKA 1873

Country: Russia. **Size:** 101 ft. in diameter, gun turret 7 ft. high.
It was a circular gun ship.

Vice-Admiral Popov of the Imperial Russian Navy was much taken with the ideas of John Elder, a Glasgow shipbuilder, who had made designs for a stable, round ship with a flat bottom. Realizing that they would be ideal for the defense of the shallow waters of the Black Sea coasts, Popov ordered two of these ships and they became known as Popoffkas, or little Popovs. Launched in 1873, they carried a revolving gun turret with two 11-ton guns. Although the Popoffkas were ideally stable, the six steam-driven propellers caused handling problems. These circular ships were said to spin like a top, and no more were ordered.

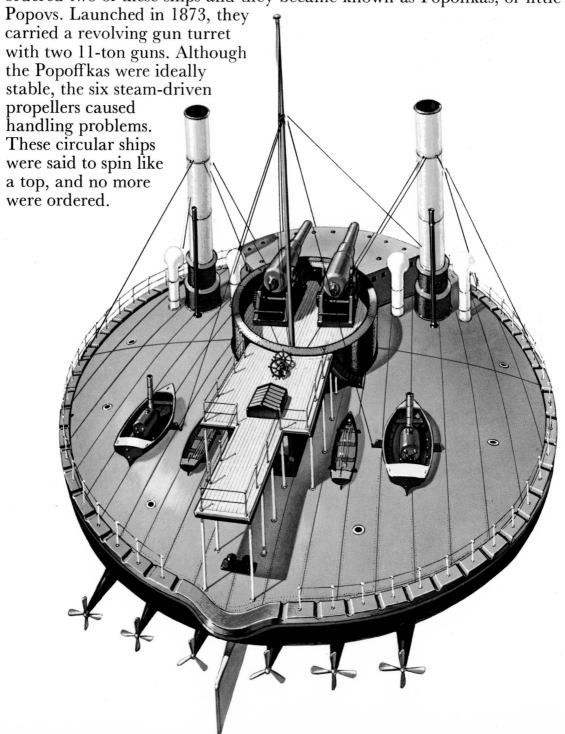

RHONE TUG
1870

Country: France. **Size:** wheel 20 ft. in diameter.
It was a river tug with a huge spiked wheel.

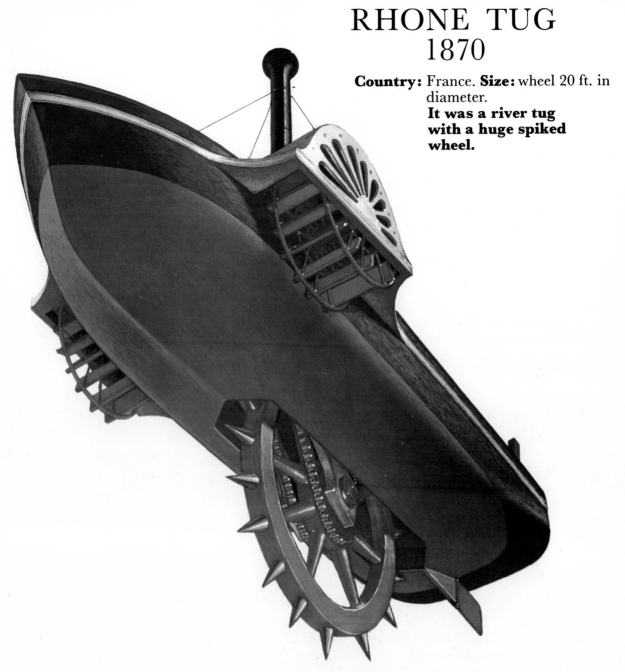

The great Rhone River which rises in Switzerland and runs from Lake Geneva and across France to the Mediterranean, is renowned for its very strong currents. In the days before steam and motor power, the boatmen who lived and worked along the riverbank had a hard time controlling the boats and barges that were then in use. This brilliantly successful boat was based on an ordinary tug with steam-driven paddles. Put into the hull, however, was this extraordinary spiked wheel, some 20 feet in diameter. As the spikes engaged with the river bottom, the chain-driven drive wheel propelled the tug forward against the strong current, up the river. However, when travelling with the current, two small engines lifted the wheel off the bottom and the craft once again became an ordinary paddle-driven tug.

MISSISSIPPI PADDLE STEAMER 1884

Country: U.S.A. **Size:** 121 ft. long, 27 ft. wide.
They were the showboats of the Mississippi.

These flat-bottomed steam boats, with their huge paddle at the back and wooden decks, are quite unmistakable. Since their introduction in 1811 more than 5,000 have been built. Apart from carrying cargo and passengers, they became the 'showboats' of the 1870's and companies of actors, singers and dancers travelled the river on these boats, collecting large audiences along the banks. Mark Twain set the seal on their popularity when he wrote about the romance of the paddle steamers in his tales. He himself was a river pilot and his love of the river is forever fixed in the name he chose as a writer. 'Mark Twain!' was the cry of the leadsman announcing that the shallow waters of the Mississippi River were two feet deep.

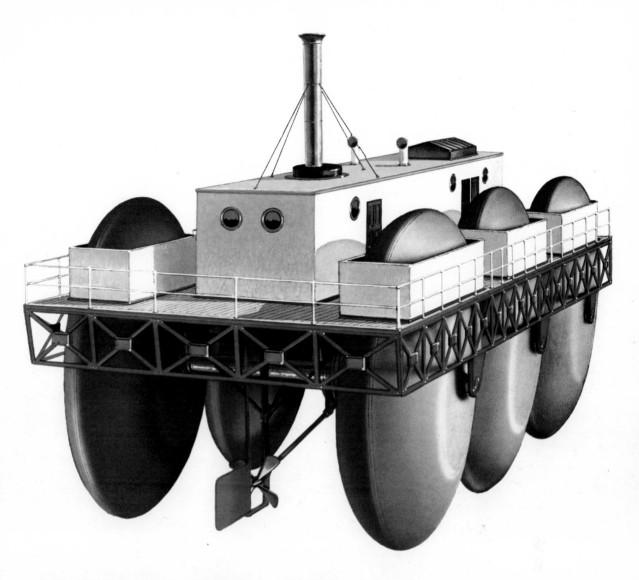

ROLLER SHIP 1896

Country: France. **Size:** 126 ft. long, 40 ft. wide. Hollow floats 33 ft. in diameter; hub 10 ft. wide.
It had six huge rotating floats.

Long before anyone else had built hydrofoils or hovercraft, a Frenchman, Ernest Bazin, thought of building a ship that would float above the water. He built a large steel structure on which a wooden deck was laid. This was then lifted 10 feet out of the water by six huge circular floats which, when rotated, gave the craft its main forward propulsion. The sizeable deck had room for passengers and crew as well as the bridge, engine room and galley. Although Bazin had built his highly experimental ship to make the channel crossing between France and England, the ship never saw service. She was hard to handle and there were many faults in the final design. The most serious was that she never came near to reaching the expected speed of 30 knots and thus further plans for this unusual ship were abandoned.

THOMAS LAWSON
1902

Country: U.S.A. **Size:** 375 ft. long, 50 ft. wide.
It was the only 7-masted schooner ever built.

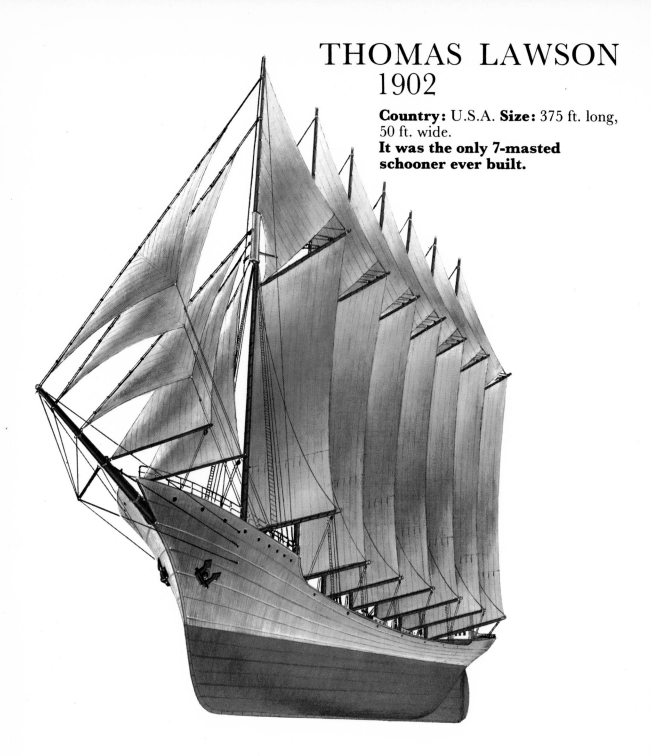

This is an example of a schooner built to compete with steamships, at a time when sailing ships were rapidly disappearing. There were five-masters, then six and then this schooner, the only one of her kind ever built, with seven masts. The Thomas Lawson was an extraordinary, top-heavy vessel. Her hull was built of steel, and steam-powered machinery was needed to hoist the enormous spread of canvas sail—an area of 4,444 square yards. Alas, she was a complete flop, being sluggish and difficult to handle. No captain was happy with her and her life was short and disastrous. She was lost with nearly all her crew off the Scilly Isles not long after being built.

ROTOR SHIP 1924

Country: Germany.
Size: Rotors, 55 ft. high, 13 ft. in diameter.
It had three towers rotated by the wind.

Anton Flettner believed that it was possible to harness the winds to increase the speed of a ship by using methods other than sails. He managed to obtain government support for the conversion of a small cargo vessel and built three enormously tall, light, metal towers into the ship's decks, engineering them so that they revolved according to the wind direction. These rotors alone gave his boat, named the Barbara, a speed of 6 knots and when used with the engines a reasonable speed of 13 knots was reached. Fuel costs were low, but running costs proved too high. At the time, people were far more interested in engines which provided more power and which were economical to build and run.

U.S.S. ENTERPRISE
1961

Country: U.S.A. **Size:** 1,102 ft. long, 252 ft. wide and 85,350 tons. **Speed:** 35 knots.
It is the longest aircraft carrier in the world.

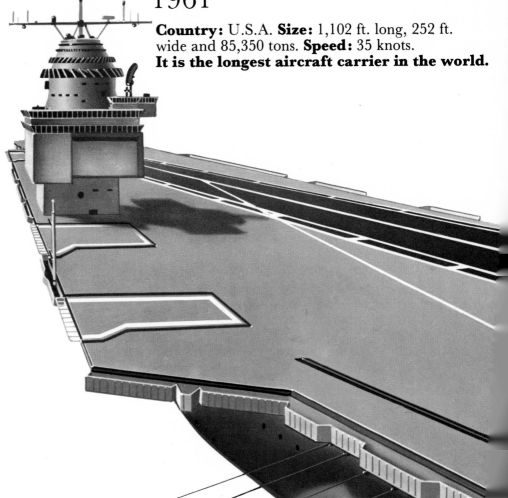

Because of their function as mobile airfields, aircraft carriers have become the largest of all warships. When launched in 1961, the Enterprise was the largest warship afloat at 85,350 tons. Capable of handling 100 aircraft, she carries a crew of some 4,600 people, including pilots, crews and their maintenance staff. Unlike the heavy, slow, armor-plated carriers of both world wars, the Enterprise has a great turn of speed, being able to reach 35 knots. Originally she was built with no armaments other than the 100 aircraft, but today she carries a defense missile system.

Perhaps the most remarkable feature of this giant warship is the fact that it is powered by nuclear energy and contains eight water-cooled reactors to drive the steam turbine engines. One of the particular advantages of these reactors is their ability to provide very intense heat in a very short space of time, thus enabling the great turbines to start quicker than conventionally powered ships. In addition, 'refuelling' need only take place at three-year intervals although food and other supplies are required more often.

The USS Enterprise is still the longest aircraft carrier in the world, but the USS Nimitz (1973) at 95,100 tons is heavier.

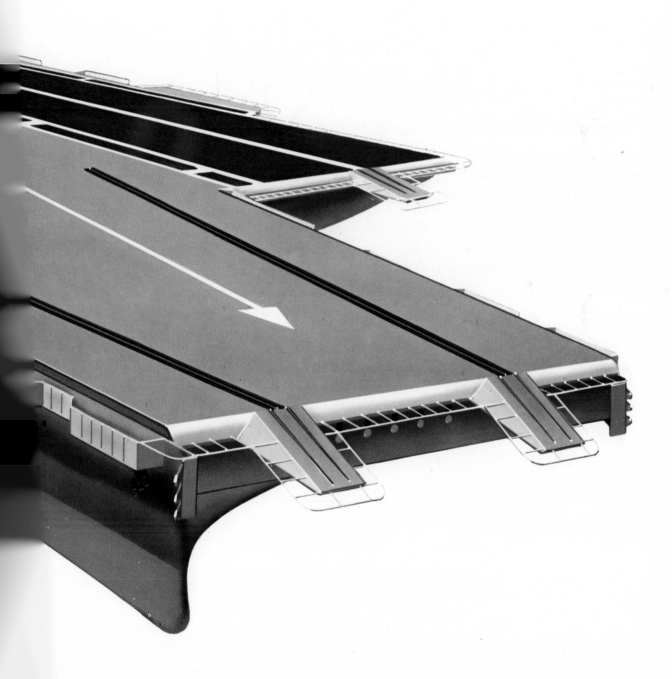

HOVERCRAFT SRN 6
1968

Country: Great Britain. **Size:** 130 ft. long,
77 ft. wide. **Top Speed:** 77 knots.
It 'floats' on a cushion of air.

Engineers had been experimenting with the idea
of a vehicle supported on a cushion of air since
1877, but it was left to an Englishman, Sir
Christopher Cockerell, to patent this
revolutionary invention. Powerful fans
create a cushion of air which is trapped
by a surrounding skirt. This allows
sufficient clearance for the craft to
travel across land or water. The
first Hovercraft cross-Channel trip
to Calais was made in 1959 on the
50th anniversary of Blériot's first
Channel flight. The craft
you see here is currently in
use as a cross-Channel car ferry
and can carry
30 cars and
254 passengers.

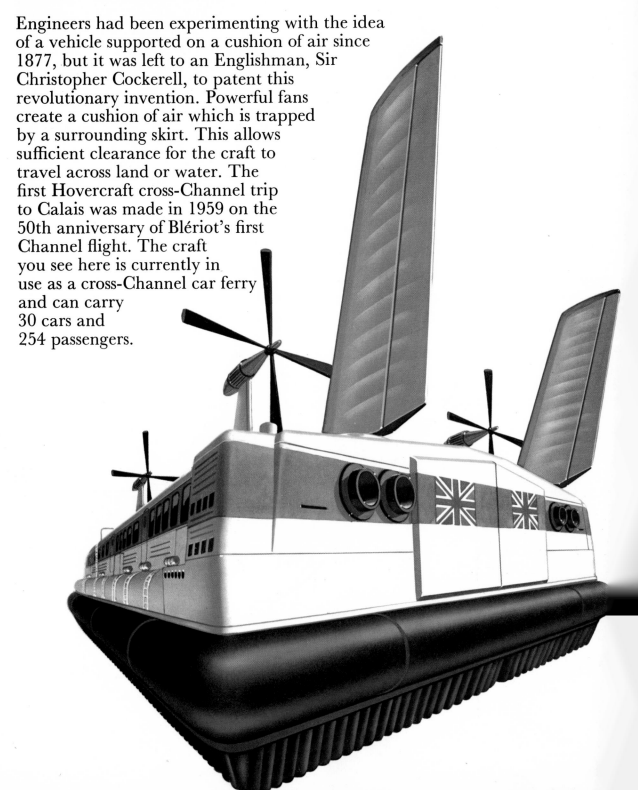

HYDROFOIL 1973

Country: Italy. **Size:** 72 ft. 2 in. long, 24 ft. 3 in. wide, including foils.
It lifts itself up on to its 'skis'.

The first Hydrofoil tests were made by a French count on the River Seine
in 1891. Both Alexander Graham Bell, the inventor of the telephone,
and the famous Wright Brothers drew up plans for such a craft. Above a
certain speed the air forces the front of the boat up on to the foils, or
skis, which you can see in the picture. As with the Bluebird (see next
page), the purpose of this is to reduce water resistance, giving a smoother
ride and greater speeds. Today there are many Hydrofoils in use and an
American naval patrol boat has reached a speed of 70 knots. The one
pictured here was built in England in 1973 and runs from Southampton
to Cowes.

CAMPBELL'S BLUEBIRD
1955–67

Country: Great Britain. **Size:** 26 ft. 4¾ in. long, 10 ft. 6 in. wide.
It was a World Speed Record-breaker.

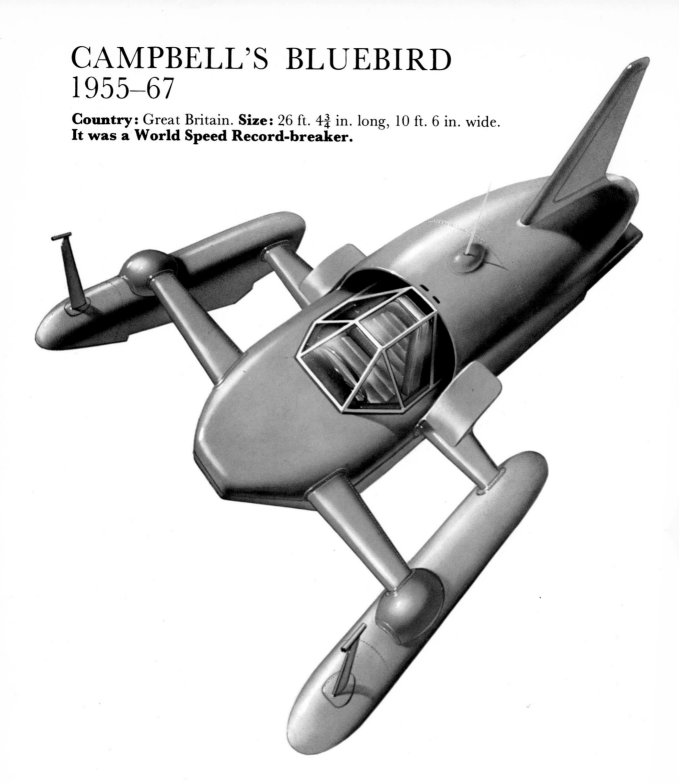

The names of Malcolm and Donald Campbell will always be linked with water speed records, as well as land speed records. Donald Campbell, with his engineer, Leo Villa, designed and built the Bluebird illustrated here. Powered by a jet engine, it had sponsons which planed along the surface of the water. This same boat broke record after record, from the first boat to reach the magic 200 m.p.h. mark to 276 m.p.h. in 1964. In 1967, on yet another record attempt Donald Campbell was killed in this Bluebird.

PLANESAIL 1968

Country: Great Britain. **Size:** 29 ft. long.
It is a trimaran using aerofoils instead of sails.

The Planesail in this picture is one of several specially developed trimarans. Instead of a mast and sails, it has upright, rigid aerofoils, similar in design to an airplane wing. By selecting the angle at which these aerofoils are turned to the wind, in the same way that sails are set, these light and fast craft are able to skim through the water. Controlled from the cabin with a steering wheel and foot controls, Planesails are ideal as cruising trimarans.

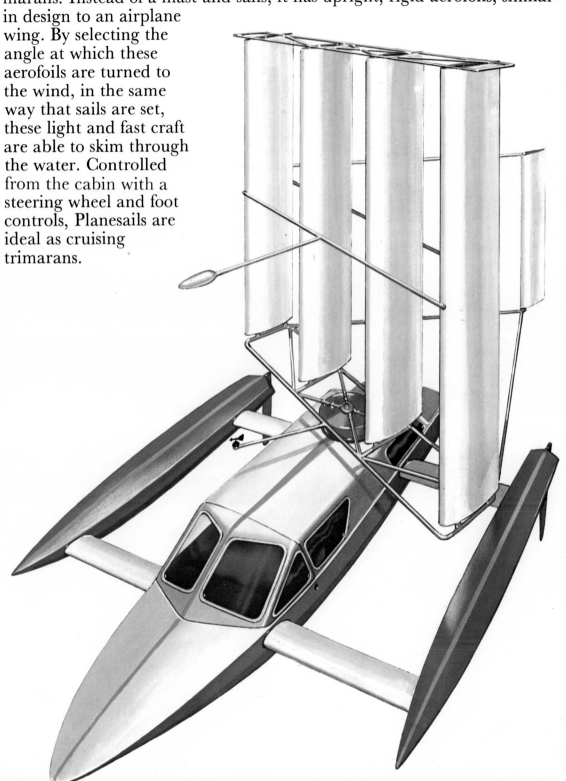

PEN DUIK IV 1964

Country: France. **Size:** 65 ft. long.
**It broke the record for the crossing of the
Atlantic by sail.**

Like the Planesail, this trimaran was developed from
the idea of the outrigger canoe (see Maori Tainui).
The Pen Duik IV is one of a series of boats of
the same name built by the well-known
French yachtsman, Eric Tabarly.
With many revolutionary ideas, she was built
of aluminium and with revolving masts.
Carrying a crew of three, she broke
the record for the fastest crossing
of the Atlantic by sail. After initial
problems as a single-handed boat,
she has now become one of
the fastest offshore sailing
boats in the world, and was
the winner of the single-
handed Transatlantic
race in 1972.

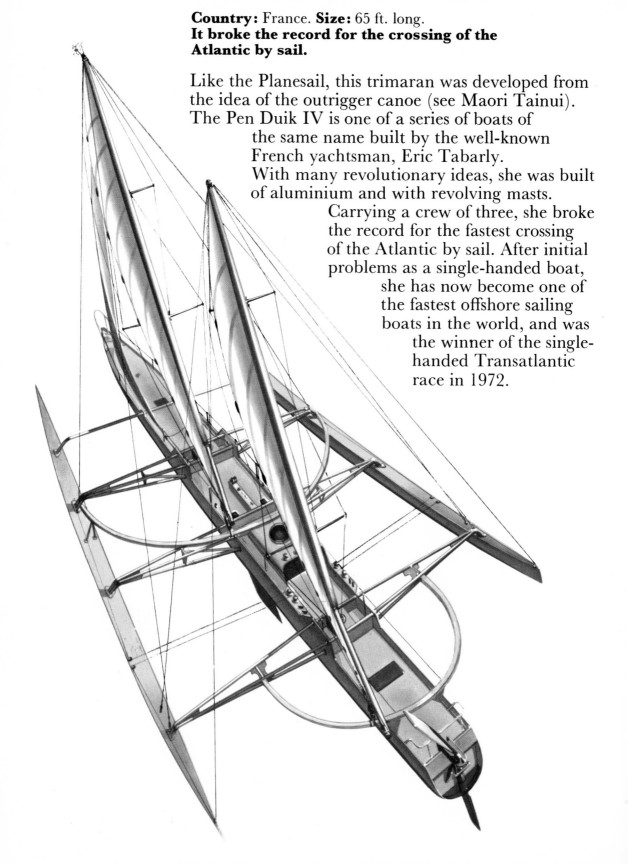

CROSSBOW 1972

Country: Great Britain. **Size:** 60 ft. and 15 ft. long, 30 ft. across.
It is one of the fastest offshore sailing craft ever built.

You will notice that the two hulls are unequal—one 60 feet
long, the other a mere 15 feet long. This means
that the Crossbow can only be sailed with the wind on the
starboard side; the mast would break off if the sails were caught
by a sudden gust on the port bow.
The helmsman sits on the tiny, secondary hull and steers with
his feet. The rest of the crew run up and down the 'plank' which
connects the two hulls, trying to keep the yacht steady and
aiming to keep the smaller hull just above the surface
of the water. Nicknamed 'The Best', this yacht won the high
speed sailing competition in 1972 with a speed
of 26.3 knots.

GLOBTIK TOKYO 1973

Country: Japan. **Size:** 1,243 ft. long, 203 ft. wide and 477,000 tons deadweight.
It is one of the largest ships ever built.

With man's need for energy, the transportation of oil has provided one of the most spectacular developments in the history of boats.
In the 1930's it was rare for a tanker to exceed 15,000 tons and yet forty years later there are plans for tankers of more than 500,000 tons! The Globtik Tokyo is the largest tanker afloat today at 477,000 tons, and, among other things, it has the largest propeller ever built. Despite the enormous size of this boat, the crew only numbers around forty.

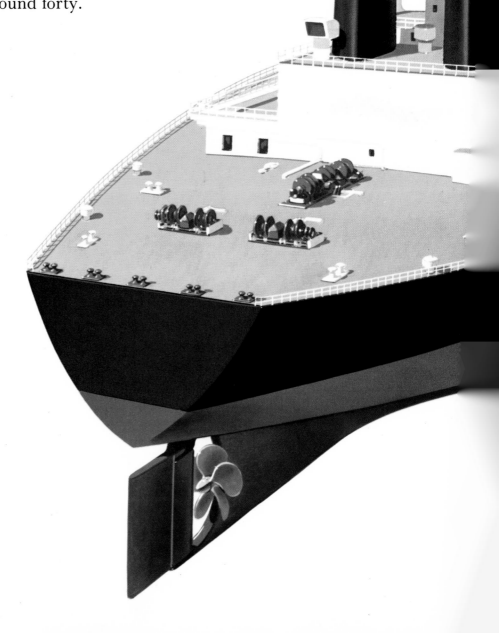

Because of their huge draught and their difficulty in turning and maneuvering, these tankers can take as much as three miles to stop. They can only dock in the really deep water harbors of the world and terminals out at sea are often constructed close to oil refineries to overcome this problem.

GLOSSARY

aerofoil: a wing-like structure, curved on the top side and flat on the bottom.

ballast: weight placed in bottom of ship to secure stability.

bow: curved fore-end of ship, from where it narrows towards the stem.

canvas, spread of: unfurled sails, usually made of coarse cotton.

conning tower: observation tower on top of the hull of a submarine.

draught: depth of water needed for ship to float safely.

freeboard: the part of the hull that is out of the water.

hull: the frame of a ship.

keel: lowest wooden or metal part of a ship.

knot: a nautical mile, 6,080 ft.

port: left-hand side of the ship.

prow: fore-part above stem of ship, usually projecting.

rigging: supporting ropes that control sails and masts.

schooner: vessel with two or more masts.

shrouds: set of ropes which support the mast.

sponson: small float or projection which increases boat's stability in the water.

starboard: right-hand side of a ship.

stem: the upright piece of metal or timber at the front of a ship to which the ship's sides are joined.

stern: the same as the stem, but at the back of the ship.

trawls: fishing nets used by sea-going fishing boats.

trimaran: three-hulled yacht.

yacht: light sailing vessel, usually specially built for racing or pleasure cruising.